30 Days of Inspiration

#Be Inspired
#Be Ready
#Believe

Tarey D Meeks

Meek & HUMBLE PUBLISHING

#Be Inspired #Be Ready #Believe   30 Days of Inspiration

Copyright © 2016 by Tarey D Meeks
McKinney, Texas 75069

ISBN- 978-0-9978878-1-5

Cover Design by Moore Designs

Published in McKinney, Texas, by Meek & Humble Publishing.

Library of Congress Cataloging-in-Publication Data:

Meeks, Tarey, 1963-
    Be Inspired Be Ready Believe/ Tarey D. Meeks

Join the online Facebook community for Tarey's Inspirational Page at
https://www.facebook.com/tareysinspirations/

Table of Contents

Acknowledgements   7

Introduction   9

Day 1   A Repentant Heart   11

Day 2   Be Vigilant   13

Day 3   Surrender   15

Day 4   Faithfulness   17

Day 5   Sacrifice   19

Day 6   Deny the Flesh   21

Day 7   Wisdom   23

Day 8   Let Go, Let God   25

Day 9   One Love   27

Day 10   Stand Strong   29

Day 11   Accountability   31

Day 12   Live Holy   33

Day 13   Submission   35

Day 14   In His Presence   37

Day 15   Holy Spirit Power   39

Day 16   Perserverance   41

Day 17   Obedience   43

Day 18   Let your Light Shine   46

Day 19   Self-Evaluation   49

Day 20   Righteousness   51

Day 21   Transparency   53

Day 22   Dedication   55

Day 23   Depend on God   57

Day 24   Daily Instructions   59

Day 25   Made in His Image   61

Day 26   Wise Choices   63

Day 27   Acknowledge God   66

Day 28   Quick to Listen   69

Day 29   The Truth   71

Day 30   One Day at a Time   74

Acknowledgements

I DEDICATE 30 DAYS OF INSPIRATION TO MY MOTHER,

Athelgra Neville Gabriel

You have always been a constant source of encouragement to pursue my writing endeavors and to

soar beyond my wildest dreams. You were always available for me no matter how big or small the

situation was. I know that you desired great things for me and I am grateful that you continued

to push me to my limits. I give glory and honor to God for blessing me with this gift and enabling

me to use it for his glory. Without the Lord on my side, none of this would be possible. Mom, this

book is the result of continual prayer and commitment to God and the work of the Kingdom and

the fact that you believed in me. I thank you and I love you

to infinity and beyond.

Introduction

Each day that you awake, can be an opportunity for something great or something not so great to take place in your life. If you purpose in your mind to begin your day by seeking the Lord and asking that His will be done, then you are more than likely headed toward something great. The writings in this inspirational can be the added motivation needed to start the morning. Neither of us are immune to the negativity surrounding us, but we do have the power of the Holy Spirit within us, to govern ourselves appropriately. Every day is another chance to do just what it is that you are called to do. Reading these daily inspirations will encourage you to **Be Inspired**, equip you to **Be Ready**, and empower you to **Believe** that today is that day.

Day 1

A Repentant Heart

God expects us to prove that we have repented of our sins and have turned to Him by the way that we live our lives. He is not listening to what we say but He's watching our lifestyle. God is ready to separate the wheat from the chaff; that is, separating those who have taken heed to the call of God from those who remain unrepentant, and simpler, the true worshippers from those only giving lip service. It is written, not everyone who calls out to Him, Lord, Lord, will enter into the Kingdom of Heaven. Only those who actually DO the will of the Father. Today I pray that none of us deceives ourselves, and we do a self-examination as it pertains to our salvation. I pray that we all understand that God sees all things and knows all things and we cannot fool Him. I pray that we all will enter in, In Jesus Name, Amen!!

#abideinHisword   #hideHisWordinyourheart

#BeReady   Luv Y'all

Your Thoughts

Day 2

Be Vigilant

The enemy realizes that his time is almost over. He has thrown all caution to the wind and anything goes. He is creating illusions trying to deceive us into believing his lies as the truth. Because of who we are and what we stand for, the enemy is in full force and everything of the world hates us and is against us. The enemy is going above and beyond to tempt us and to trick us into denying Christ. Take heed to the quickening of the Spirit within you, warning of possible traps set by the enemy. We don't want to get caught off guard and fall by the wayside. Today I pray that we remain vigilant so as to not be devoured by the enemy. I pray that we stand firm in God's grace and not fall to the wiles of the enemy. In Jesus Name, Amen!

#prowlinglikearoaringlion

#BeREadY   Luv Y'all!!

Your Thoughts

Day 3

Surrender

It's one thing to be struggling in an area of our faith walk. However, it's a totally different obstacle when we're in denial about even having the issue. The more we profess to be delivered from the stronghold, and yet continue to indulge in those guilty pleasures when we think no one is watching, the more we are setting ourselves up to be destroyed by the enemy. The word says a double minded man is unstable in all his ways. That means if we're being deceitful about one thing, the Lord can't trust us in anything. We're not fooling anyone but ourselves. Remember God will not be mocked. The reason we don't see any breakthrough in our situation is because we're playing on the devil's playground. We can't have it both ways. We're either hot or cold. Today I pray that if any of us finds ourselves with this dilemma, we be allowed to remove our own covers and repent. I pray that God's grace be upon us. I pray that we decide that enough is enough and we deny our flesh so the Spirit man can rise up. I declare that today, the enemy's hold is annihilated in the name of Jesus. I pray the Lord strengthens us to break free. In Jesus name, Amen!

#ifyougottasneaktodoitushouldntdoit
#checkyourselfbeforeyouwreckyourself
#BeREadY   Luv Y'all!

Your Thoughts

Day 4

Faithfulness

Our dedication to God and the building of His Kingdom are obvious signs that depict our faith. Our measure of faith begins when we repent; when we transform our hearts and minds by turning away from sin and toward God. Without that transformation it is impossible to live a life in obedience to God. For those of us who can live according to God's will, He promises His blessings. It is our faith in God that pleases Him. It is our faith that draws us nearer to God. It is that same faith that ignites the desire in us to obey God and His Word. Today I pray that the burning fire consumes everything in us that is not pleasing to God and is hindering us from saying Yes to Him. I pray that we have an experience with God today that touches us so deeply that we fall to our knees immediately to ask for forgiveness and ask what must we do to be in one mind with Christ. In Jesus Name, Amen!

#thesubstanceofthingshopedfor
#theevidenceofthingsnotseen
#gotFaith   #BeREadY   Luv Y'all!!

Your Thoughts

Day 5

Sacrifice

Jesus didn't die for us to fail. In fact, the purpose of His death, was for all of us to have the opportunity to live with Him eternally in Heaven. His death made it possible for a wretch like me to be redeemed and reconciled back to the Father. His death was a price that was paid for our ransom. His death was a setup for us to come back. His death was to give us a clean start. For all that He endured for us, is He asking too much of us? Are we going to allow His death to be in vain? Today I pray that each of us realizes how indispensable Jesus' sacrifice was for humanity. I pray that we all wake up before it's too late. In Jesus name, Amen!!

#gaveupHislifeforUS #IJS #nogreaterlovethanHis

#BeREadY Luv Y'all!!

Your Thoughts

Day 6

Deny the Flesh

It is understandable that being called to discipleship is hard, but what great achievement ever came easily? Following Jesus requires a total commitment to be able to deny our flesh, and that is why Jesus extends His grace to us. We have to follow Him without being ashamed to be who He called us to be. Regardless to how painful it might be; we have to eliminate anything that will distract us from following through with our promise. We must trust in God completely and our loyalty must be to Him, forsaking ALL others. Today I pray that we rely on the Holy Spirit to strengthen us to pick up our cross to follow Christ. I pray that we are bold to proclaim the Good news to all that we meet. I pray that we all are members of the family of God, saved from judgement and we receive eternal life. In Jesus name, Amen!

#denyyourself #itsadailywalk #BeREadY

Luv Y'all!!

Your Thoughts

Day 7

Wisdom

There are many who have heard the Word about Jesus, but still struggle with knowing who He really is. In John Chapter 6, even the crowds were not sure what to make of Him. Some wanted to follow Him, while others wanted Him arrested. It is even written in John 16:12-13, that the disciples didn't really come to understand Jesus' significance until they had received the Holy Spirit. There are those of us still living in darkness that can't understand the realness of God. They are not in position to receive the divine revelation of who He is. Some have come to love the darkness to a point where they run from the light. Only through the Holy Spirit will we see God as He is. Today I pray that we are able to push through the dark places in our lives to see the light. I pray that the power of the Holy Spirit penetrates our hardened hearts and removes the scales from our eyes so we can receive the light. I pray that we come into the full knowledge of Christ and let Him into our lives and never turn back, in Jesus Name, Amen!

#inallthygettinggetunderstanding   #BeREadY
Luv Y'all!!

Your Thoughts

Day 8

Let Go Let God

No matter how often we would like to take matters into our own hands and think that we are in control, that couldn't be further from the truth. We think that we have it within our own power to determine how a situation is going to turn out. Even though our decisions play a role in the event of things, the will of God will prevail. In every situation, God decides if, when and to whom He extends His mercy. As believers, who are trusting in God wholeheartedly, we can confidently say that all things work together for the good of those who love God and are called according to His purpose for us. Today I pray that we don't become so full of ourselves to believe we can do it on our own. I pray that we lean and depend on the wisdom and guidance of the Holy Spirit of God, to lead us to the expected end, in Jesus name, Amen!!
#Godisincontrol   #BeREadY Luv Y'all!!

Your Thoughts

Day 9

One Love

Every believer is a member of the body of Christ and we are the church. The Holy Spirit gifts each of us for our specific ministries for the benefit of the church. Therefore, we are to be sensitive to the empowering of the Holy Spirit in everything we do. Anytime we come together, whether it's in a building or through the posts on FB, we all bring something from God to share with each other. Each person is important to the body and each person has a role to play. We are all called to be actively involved in the growth of God's church. Today I pray that every believer accepts full responsibility for their role in growing the Kingdom of God. I pray that we all use our God given gifts to edify the body of Christ. I pray that in the midst of it all, we understand that love is the one thing that brings it all together, more importantly than the gifts. In Jesus Name, Amen!!

#sowebeingmanyareONEbodyinChrist

#apartfromLoveourgiftshavenovalue
#BeREadY   Luv Y'all!!

Your Thoughts

Day 10

Stand Strong

I just feel the need to reiterate that the devil is real and he embodies evil. His main purpose is to obstruct everything that we do in the name of the Lord. He is very serious about his job, and he is always prowling like a roaring lion to see whom he can devour. The enemy will always try to expose us to his destructive powers, but we, as believers must stand firm and resist the devil. Anyone who is not a believer is susceptible to him and to sin. Oh, but God! He came to put an end to the enemy's plans. Everything the enemy contrives against us, God turns it around for our good. The Holy Spirit within us is greater than the enemy, so we need not worry. The power of the devil is no match for the power of God! Today I pray that we remain dressed in the armor of God to always BE READY! I pray that we never let our guard down and we continue asking, seeking and knocking. I pray for the strength to fight to the finish, in Jesus name, Amen!!

#dontgetcomfortable #initotwinit
#BeREadY Luv Y'all!!

Your Thoughts

Day 11

Accountability

We are all accountable to God for our sins. Be assured, that He shows His anger against all who are sinful, and those who cover up the truth by their unrighteous living, in spite of their knowledge of the truth. When we are consistently being stubborn and refusing to turn away from our sin, we are only storing up punishment for ourselves. The Word says, God will judge everyone according to what they have done. He gives eternal life to those who continue doing good, but His wrath will pour down on those who live for themselves. The day is coming when God, through Christ Jesus, will judge everyone's secret life. Romans 2

Today I pray that we live the truth that we have been made aware of. I pray that the very thought of displeasing God, promptly reverts our minds to the sacrifice He made for us. I pray that we all constantly examine ourselves, whether we be in faith, In Jesus name Amen!

#dontgetcaughtslipping #BeREady Luv Y'all!!

Your Thoughts

Day 12

Live Holy

The calling that God has on the life of the believer is very crucial. He calls us to live as His holy people. Although it may be difficult, He has given us everything we need to sustain ourselves. We have the ability to be distinctly different from the rest of the world with the power of the Holy Spirit within us. We are to keep ourselves pure in every aspect of the word. Pure in our hearts, thoughts and pure in our bodies. Our bodies are a sanctuary of the living God and we belong to Him. Let's keep that in mind as we walk in our calling and we endeavor to keep holy. Today I pray that we realize the importance of adhering to the requirements of being a follower and believer of Christ. I pray that each day we set out with the intention to follow through with every command given to us by our Lord and Savior Jesus Christ. I pray that we be so totally sold out, that nothing can turn us back, in Jesus Name, Amen!!

#beholybecauseHeisholy #BeREadY   Luv Y'all!

Your Thoughts

Day 13

Submission

Each day we must submit ourselves to the Lord. The more we allow Him to cleanse us and remove everything that is not like Him, we become more like Him and we are better able to perceive His presence. Our hearts begin to desire Him more and He becomes that much more attainable to us. He is eager to fulfill our every desires as we look unto Him in total dependency. Besides there is nothing that we could need or want, that He is not already aware of. Today I pray that the Lord is the first thought on our minds. I pray that we become childlike in our faith in Him. I pray that we place ourselves in the potter's hands as He molds us to be His masterpiece, In Jesus name, Amen!!

#Godisable #opentheEyesofourheart #BeREadY Luv Y'all!!

Your Thoughts

Day 14

In His Presence

There are times when we may need to just get to a quiet place and lay in the presence of the Lord. It may not necessarily be a time when there's any havoc going on, but we may just feel an urging in our spirit. We should recognize it as the Lord wanting to spend more time with us. He comes looking for us. I know it may be difficult to get that quiet time alone, but any opportunity that is taken advantage of, will be a joyful one. Today I pray that we all commit to setting aside at least 10 minutes per day to sit in the Lord's Presence. I pray that He will show up and love on you like never before. I pray that we will never again say we don't have the time but purposefully make the time. I pray that we all fall in love with Jesus as much as He loves us, In Jesus name, Amen!

#taketimetobequiet #bestillandknow #fullnessofJoy
Psalm 16:11   #BeREadY   Luv Y'all!!

Your Thoughts

Day 15

Holy Spirit Power

God was very deliberate when He left His Holy Spirit with us. His Spirit is filled with the power that is needed to sustain us in the holy life we are expected to live. Only with God's Spirit in us, are we able to resist our sinful nature. The Holy Spirit acts as our conscience to help us decipher right from wrong. It is in our nature, that our hearts are wicked and deceitful, and without the power of the Holy Spirit within us, our hearts can't be changed and we will be unable to do the things that please God. Today I pray that we welcome the Holy Spirit into our lives so that a total transformation can take place. I pray that we are willing and ready for the metamorphosis to begin. I pray for the strength to go through the necessary changes no matter how painful it may get. I pray that we all know how detrimental it would be to ourselves and those connected to us, if we do not. In Jesus name, Amen!

#withouttheHolySpiritwecandonothing

#youshallreceivepower #BeREadY   Luv Y'all!!

Your Thoughts

Day 16

Perseverance

Endurance is the ability to stand firm during an unpleasant or difficult situation without yielding. As believers, we may be subject to unsurmountable difficulties and hardships, because of our spiritual commitment. We have to dig in with all that we have inside of us to hold firmly to what we believe without becoming unsteady. These are things we are faced with when waiting in anticipation for the things that God has promised us. In order to continue growing in our spirituality and in our holiness, we must be obedient to the voice of God, and when we slip, we must prepare for God to discipline us. All of this is imperative for our witness to be effective. Today I pray that we all can stand the test of time. I pray that we all be joyful in hope, patient in affliction and faithful in prayer. I pray that we all are so focused on the prize that nothing is too hard for us to bear, in Jesus name, Amen!! Romans 12:12

#sufferingproducesperserverance□□□ #BeREadY□
□□ Luv Y'all!!

Your Thoughts

Day 17

Obedience

Can you imagine your name not being in the lamb's Book of Life? The one's whose name is not in the Lamb's Book of Life is thrown into the Lake of Fire. I don't know about you, but I am determined to hear well done my good and faithful servant. At the end of all this, I am looking forward to hearing my name being called and spending eternity in Heaven with the Father. God's Word gives us lots of promises of life everlasting, however, it also contains strict warnings, that if we don't take heed to them, we are headed to the lake of fire. Most of us tend to overlook the warnings because we are so comfortable in doing the things that we want to do and that make us feel in control with a sense of security. We fail to realize that the warnings only direct us to being obedient and faithful and through adhering to those instructions, we are provided security from God and are placed on the path to righteousness. Furthermore, all of the promises of God are received only through our obedience and faithfulness to the Word of God. The

thing that brings judgement upon us is our disobedience. Today I pray that we don't allow the enemy to keep us closed off to correction. I pray that we understand the relevance of the warnings and we choose life over death. I pray that obeying God becomes more important than being in control of our own lives. In Jesus Name, Amen!!
Matthew 25:46
#dontbeblottedout #therighteousgointoeternallife #BeREadY   Luv Y'all!!

Your Thoughts

Day 18

Let Your Light Shine

Believers should expect the world to be unfriendly toward us. The fact that we are living obedient to God makes us susceptible to their discrimination and mockery. Even in that, God has a plan for us. As we suffer for Christ, we are brought closer in relationship with Him. We can also be confident that we will have the victory and will enjoy the glory with God. We must always commit to doing right no matter what we may be facing. Sometimes the things we go through can be so overwhelming that we are tempted to use it as an excuse for sinning. It is in that instance of overcoming that it is possible to win over the unbeliever. It is in the times when our enemies rightfully deserve a harsh word or harsh treatment and we choose to respond lovingly, that we have the opportunity to witness. We have just made living for Christ respectable in their eyes. The important thing to remember is that God controls all the circumstances in our lives and we never have to fear that anything is going to come our way that God is not already aware of. Today I pray that we let our light shine before men that they will see our good works and glorify our Father which is in heaven. I pray that we have the attitude of Christ when it comes to going through knowing that we have the victory. In Jesus name Amen!!

#tosufferforChristisgain
#dontletyourgoodbeevilspokenof
#BeREadY   Luv Y'all!!

Your Thoughts

Day 19

Self Evaluation

The journey of every believer is an individual course that is designed just for them. No path is identical and it's very seldom that two may be in the same place at the same time. The only definite corresponding point is the final destination; contingent upon the fact that each believer remains on course. This also means that our relationship with God differs. For example, one believer may feel that it's okay to listen to secular music, or have a daiquiri every now and again, while on the other hand, another believer may feel that engaging in those activities would desecrate their commitment. The deeper the relationship, the more intent our convictions are. Today I pray that each believer is continually evaluating their own relationship with God and rightly dividing the word of truth. I pray that we remain compassionate toward each other, respecting the growth of each other while continuing to encourage and uplift each other. I pray that we all reach that expected end. In Jesus name Amen!! Romans 14

#finishyourrace #destinationEternity
#howdeepisyourlove   #BeREadY
Luv Y'all!!
=

Your Thoughts

Day 20

Righteousness

The bible speaks of an end time resurrection, where the dead will be resurrected. This resurrection will not be the same for all. The resurrection will reveal the true nature of a person and an account must be given to God. There are those who will be raised to experience a new life and those who will be raised to experience degradation. The difference is based on the morals, ethics and spiritual character of each individual. Have we been morally, ethically and spiritually renewed? Those in the first group will experience everlasting life; not referring to as much to the length, but more to the quality of life, whereas, those in the second group will suffer everlasting shame and disgrace. Today I pray that we resolve in our hearts and minds to be refined, cleansed and made pure before God. I pray that we will be found righteous in the sight of God. I pray that we are living the lives that we speak about and we will be amongst

those rejoicing in heaven, in Jesus name, Amen!!
Daniel 12

#TheEnd   #BeREadY   Luv Y'all!

Your Thoughts

Day 21

Transparency

Some of us may be guilty of pretending that things are better than they really are. We hide behind masks to avoid embarrassment, to please others or to paint a better picture of ourselves. Wearing masks can be unhealthy in our spiritual walk because it hinders our growth and it becomes difficult to let God in. The good thing about it is that God doesn't see the mask. He sees us as He created us. As we diligently seek Him, we get to a point where we recognize that we are wearing masks and He in turn gives us the strength to remove them, allowing us to see ourselves as He sees us. Today I pray that we accept the challenge to look ourselves in the mirror and confront those issues we are not too pleased with. I pray that we allow God to heal and restore our wounded hearts. I pray that we all see the warrior, the conqueror and the victor as we were created to be, in Jesus Name, Amen!!

#trueidentity #wearewhoGodsaysweare #BeREadY

Luv Y'all!!

Your Thoughts

Day 22

Dedication

The lifestyle of a Christian believer is not one to be taken lightly. Nothing about our commitment to the Kingdom of God is casual. Anything happening outside of the will of God is under the control of the enemy. Just as serious as God is about saving us, the enemy is just as serious about taking each of us down with him; and I mean that literally. We should take it that serious also. Before we partake in any activity, conversation or relationship, we need to seek God. Any place the enemy can find a way in, he will take it. We have to check our personal feelings at the door and allow God to take care of any backlash we may face because of the decisions we have to make to maintain our salvation. Today I pray that we all realize that the enemy does not sleep and he is playing for keeps. I pray that each day we take on the full armor of God, so that we will be able to resist in the evil day. In Jesus name, Amen!

#remaininthewillofGod
#dontplaywiththedevil   #BeREadY   Luv Y'all!!

Your Thoughts

Day 23

Depend on God

We can never put our guard down and take a chance on missing God. Every step we take needs to be led by God. There are moments when we feel confident enough to move on our own accord. It is then that we make ourselves vulnerable to the enemy because then, God is not obligated to protect us outside of His will. Some of us find it easy to smile and thank God when all is going well, but when things are going haywire, we tend to lose focus on God. We'd rather lash out on who hurt us instead of giving God praise anyhow. This is just how quickly we can get off track and end up on the wide road. Today I pray that our steps are ordered by God. I pray that we have the tenacity to bless and praise God in the midst of whatever is going on. I pray that His hands of protection stay upon each of us and we in turn lean on His hands. in Jesus Name, Amen!!

#giveittoGod #Hecanhandleit #BeREady Luv Y'all!!

Your Thoughts

Day 24

Daily Instructions

As believers, we should try to make sure that before we start our day, that we listen to God for instructions. Some days we may hear His voice immediately, but on other days, it may be quiet. On those days, we can just do the normal routine and go about doing our usual errands, but still keep our hearts and minds on God. No matter if He has something specific for us to do or not, He still wants to know that we're always available. During the course of what seems like a normal day, we still have to look to Him for direction. This act lets God know that we trust Him. Today I pray that we get into the habit of waiting to hear from God before we move. I pray that we deem it a necessity to get guidance from God in everything we do. I pray that we purpose in our hearts to love God as much as He loves us. In Jesus Name, Amen!!

#bequicktohear #obeythevoiceoftheLord

#Hewillinstructyouinthewaytogo
#BeREadY   Luv Y'all!!

Your Thoughts

Day 25

Made in His Image

There isn't anything as repulsive to God as sin. In all of His holiness, it cannot coexist with Him. By the same token, as believers, being made in His image, that should be true for us too. God expects us to emulate that same holiness and disdain for sin. In those human moments that we sometimes fall privy to, God has extended forgiveness toward us. However, that forgiveness is only extended to the truly repentant. For those who are not, they can expect His judgment. Thank God that His judgment is not immediate as it was in the Old Testament days. Today I pray for a spirit of holiness to fall across the land. I pray that we all grab hold to its essence and allow it to permeate into our souls. I pray that we uphold everything that is of God and anything that's meant to tarnish us, we are able to rebuke it and purge ourselves of the residue. In Jesus name, Amen!!

#HolyHolyHolyistheLordofHosts

#wearesetapart #cleanseusofALLunrighteousness
#BeREadY   Luv Y'all!!

Your Thoughts

Day 26

Wise Choices

The Book of Deuteronomy clearly stated to the Israelites what God expected of them. There was a covenant made requiring them to obey God. A section of the covenant listed curses and blessings and explained that God would reward obedience and judge their disobedience. We are given the same opportunity; to comply with the Word of God or suffer the consequences. To indicate the importance of obeying, the curses received more attention than the blessings. God emphasized the curses to clarify the ramifications of wrongdoing. Looking at the history of the Israelites, it definitely demonstrates God's promise of blessings and curses. When they were faithful, He blessed them and when they rebelled, He brought judgment upon them. Today I pray that we learn the lesson that came before us. I pray that we are wise to follow the Word of God making the clear choice of blessings over curses. I pray that the grace of God gives us new mercies to receive blessings that He promised in Jesus name, Amen!

#GodkeepsHispromises
#obeyHisvoiceandHewillbeourGod
#BeREadY Luv Y'all!!

Your Thoughts

Day 27

Acknowledge God

God gives each of us gifts and talents to be used in the
Kingdom for His glory. Most times these gifts and
talents are things that are natural to us and we love
doing them. The danger in this is that sometimes we
can get so involved in doing these things that we tend
to push God to the side. I'm speaking of my personal
experience. I began by praying and seeking God for
my plan and purpose. As I began working, I saw that I
was becoming so engrossed in making sure that
was being done, and I wasn't spending as much time
as before with God. The word tells us He is a jealous
God and nothing should come before Him; not even
the work we are doing for the Kingdom. Today I pray
that we all keep things in perspective and return to our
first love. I pray that we always remember to
reverence God above all things and we don't allow
anything else to become our God. I pray that we
acknowledge that it is God who gives us the ability to

do what we do and without Him we can do nothing.
In Jesus name, Amen!!
2 Cor 3:5
#forHeknowstheplansHehasforus
#ouradequacyisfromGod
#BeREadY   Luv Y'all!!

Your Thoughts

Day 28

Quick to Listen

God is always speaking to His people. We have to have a desire to hear Him and position ourselves for the moments. His voice is like a whisper and if you are not intently listening, you will miss it. We must learn to be sensitive to the Holy Spirit to know when God is trying to communicate with us. God has specific instructions for this season that we must not miss. Only those who are inclined to be all that God has called them to be and do, will receive what God has for them. Today I pray that we don't miss God in this season. I pray that nothing is more important than time with God. I pray that we listen to the urging of the Holy Spirit and be available to hear from God. I pray that we all hear the clear instructions for the days to come in Jesus Name, Amen!!

#quietlywaitforthesalvationoftheLord
#hethathasearstohearlethimhear
#thosewhohunger&thirst4Righteousnessshallbefilled

#BeREadY   Luv Y'all!!

Your Thoughts

Day 29

The Truth

Some of us are not taking God at His word. We are not truly believing that He can do all that His word says He can. If we were, we would not be in the situations that we find ourselves in. There can be a struggle to wrap our humanly finite minds around something so amazing, but we must learn to push through our simple mindsets to say, "ok God, I trust you." Begin to speak what His word says about us, our lives, our families, our finances, our health, our marriages and our ministries. When God says all things work together for the good of those who love Him and are the called according to His purpose, let's make sure that we show Him that we love Him by obeying Him and then, expect things to work together for our good. Don't look at what the enemy wants us to see, but see what God promised. Today I pray that we lift our hands and surrender it all to God. I pray that we take the Word of God as the truth that it is and apply it to our life situations. I pray that the enemy is defeated in every attempt he makes to destroy us. I pray that we are all made free by the Word of God, in Jesus name, Amen!! #speakthosethingsthatbenotasthoughtheyare #BeREadY Luv Y'all!!

Your Thoughts

Day 30

One Day at a Time

No matter how much we plan for the future, we must still seek God for guidance. We must never permit ourselves to get too far ahead of God. It is meant for us to take each day as it comes and allow God to order our steps. The Word says that He gives us our daily bread, which means that He gives us what we need for the day and doesn't want us to worry about tomorrow. That's how dependent upon Him He wants us to be. I know there are things that need to be done in advance, but in the midst of doing that, we must make sure that we are listening for further instructions. We may have planned an event to take place at a certain place and time, but nothing seems to be going right. This could be an ideal moment to sit back and ask God what we need to do; what is our next step. He wants to be involved in every aspect of our lives; EVERY aspect. Today I pray that we humble ourselves to seek God for everything. I pray that we truly understand that God already has a plan for each of us, that if we follow His plan, it will work for our good. I pray that we learn to trust God to the point where we are like babes looking to our Father, in Jesus Name Amen!!

#givenothoughtforthemorrow
#seekye1sttheKingdomofGod
#onedayatatime   #BeReadY   Luv Y'all

Your Thoughts

www.ingramcontent.com/pod-product-compliance
Lightning Source LLC
Chambersburg PA
CBHW071630040426
42452CB00009B/1573

R.E.D.

RESIST EVERY DEMON
AND HE WILL FLEE

SPIRITUAL WARFARE GUIDE AND PRAYER
BOOK

APOSTLE JULIA D. FORD

R.E.D Resist Every Demon and He Will Flee:
Spiritual Warfare Guide and Prayer Book
Copyright © October 2013
By Apostle Julia D. Ford

Published in the United States of America by ChosenButterflyPublishing
LLC

www.cb-publishing.com

Editor: Living by Design
Photographer: Bj Shores and Shooterz Photoz
Cover Layout: The Wilson Concept

.

ISBN 978-0-9831637-8-7

First Edition Printing

Printed In the United States of America
October 2013

For more information about this author please visit:

For bookings and speaking engagements email
jdfthegeneral@aol.com